Bird Song

A collection of stories, told by the beautiful wings that carry them.

jodi hills

TRISTAN Publishing

Minneapolis

To Kristi —
My forever —
friend —
I love you —
Laura
8-8-17

For Josh and Mamma -

When my nephew was three, or four, he had not yet subscribed to the social pressures of carrying a tune. He knew he loved music. He knew he loved his grandmother, my mother. He didn't know that her piano teacher told her she was wasting her parents' money, and that she grew up, without the confidence of a voice. But she had one. And within the unjudging paneled walls of her apartment on Jefferson Street, he would turn up the radio, and shout with all of his joy-filled heart, "Sing, Mamma! Sing!"

Library of Congress Cataloging-in-Publication Data

Name: Hills, Jodi, author, illustrator.
Title: Bird song : a collection of stories, told by the beautiful wings that carry them / written and illustrated by Jodi Hills.
Description: Minneapolis : TRISTAN Publishing, [2017]
Identifiers: LCCN 2016055476 | ISBN 9781939881151 (alk. paper)
Classification: LCC PS3608.I454 A6 2017 | DDC 813/.6--dc23 LC record available at https://lccn.loc.gov/2016055476

TRISTAN Publishing, Inc.
2355 Louisiana Avenue North
Golden Valley, MN 55427

Every day she decides to be happy, and sings.

I am a brave bird.

It's not like I chose to be a bird. I just was.

I don't remember leaving the nest. Was I pushed? Did I just decide to leave? Well, regardless, I am here, now, out on a limb. So these are wings. They seem like they could work. They flap ok. A bit fragile though, yes? They must work. I hope they work. I really need them to work. I see others . . . wow . . . look at them go. It looks fun. A bit terrifying. We are really up high. Really high. I could fall. I'm sure some birds have fallen. So no one tells you? Shows you? You just go? There's some trust. Do I have that much trust? Faith? Does a bird need faith to fly? I am a bird, though. I can feel it. I mean, not just to look at me. I mean I really feel it. Under all these feathers, I feel it. I was meant to fly. It feels good to say it. I AM a bird. I don't need permission. A little courage would be nice. Yes, that's right, we all have to be a little brave to just be ourselves. And I will be. I will be a brave bird. I am a brave bird.

I am ready. I am scared. I am leaving. I want to . . . I can . . . I . . . I'm flying.

As much as spring.

Something was pressing against my ribs. The pressure was not taking my breath, but threatening to, and I knew if I let it, if I gave in to it, it would take over . . . just slightly at first, like a bully at school that teases you with a tap.

I could feel the quiver in my lip, sending messages to my eyes, "You're full! You're full! Let it out." And as certain as my lips were, the lump in my throat, the pressure in my chest, all agreed, and I began to cry. I knew each year we would say goodbye to winter. We would fluff up our wings and prepare ourselves for the song . . . the sweet song of spring. But it felt good to weep for it. Weep for the change. The transition. Weep for knowing we had lost another year, and weep out of pure joy for the possibility that these new skies held. Each year, I would tell you, "But, I'm not sad . . . it's just so much inside, this love . . . "

"So it's good then? You want to do it again? Feel it again?"

Thinking of what it would be like not to have this, what some might call pain, "Oh, yes," I said. "I thank God that winter can move me as much as spring. I thank God that I can miss the seasons as they change and celebrate the new ones as they come. I thank God that I can love you this much." The tears smiled in both of their eyes now, welcoming the buds beneath them.

The bluebird replies.

Right. Right. No, I get it. It's because I'm blue. I've actually heard it before.

The bluebird of happiness. Sure, no, it's flattering. It's not everything though, you know, I mean, happiness . . .

What? Well of course I want to be happy, but I can't be pure happiness, you know. I can't make everyone happy.

Do I believe in it? That's a peculiar question. Happiness? Can you, believe in it, I mean? You can experience it, relish in it, wait for it, glow in it, but I'm not sure it's something to believe in. It's all the things that make you happy. That's what I think you can believe in.

Like what? Well, friendship. Achievement. Kindness, for instance. And there's love. Love. Probably the main thing. Now that's something to believe in. Love is there, true love, I mean, whether you're happy or not. Love sits with you, runs with you, lies with you. That's something you can hold on to. And when you feel it, truly feel it, way beyond the blue, well, that's pure joy. And joy is eternal—clouds or whatever, don't really matter. Joy is happiness mixed with soul, with heart, with peace. Now that's something to believe in. That is greater than happiness.

You liked that, did you? Well, you know what, that makes me happy. That's right, I said happy. It's still a good thing. You're smiling. That's a good color on you. No, I mean it! Be happy! That's fun! That's contagious. You can't make someone happy, but you sure can encourage it with a life well lived. Be joyful! That's a gift from within! You can always trust that, way more than you can trust happiness flying out of the blue, as it were.

And just love someone. It's going to make you so happy. And so scared. Sad sometimes. But there is nothing like it. No, there is nothing else. Nothing. No blue at all. Do you understand? Nothing. Believe that. Happiness is just wind—fun under your wings—but love, that's what will really carry you. Just love. They were both smiling.

She was here.

I loved her. People always pause here, like you are. They look at me expectantly, like I'm going to qualify it. You know, waiting for "like a mother," "a sister," "my best friend," "a lover." They, maybe you too, need it put in some category, so it all makes sense. So maybe they could have loved her? Or they weigh it against their loves. Place it in the right box, so all of our lives just make sense. But I can't do that. Did it make sense? Is love supposed to?

I can tell you this. She was never "one town over." When she was with me, she was there. Really with me. She was never in the next season. She was the hope of spring. The playfulness of summer. The melancholy of fall. And the peace of winter. That was her kindness. And oh she was kind. Please don't say, "Oh, I'm sure you were," when I say this. Please don't. I hope I was kind. "What is it like?" I would ask her. "I have no secrets," she would say, and she would laugh. Which was the secret itself, perhaps. The joy of her being. I can still hear it. The laughter in the trees. And it jumps into my heart and fills it . . . one town over from the next. How I loved her. It was her. Not me. She was love. I was lucky enough to live in it.

I hope she thought of me that way, even a little . . . I mean, as kind. What a gift she gave me, showing me, how someone can be like that. No, don't look at me like you're sure. Who can be sure? Love isn't certainty. It's only a presence. She was here. And I loved her.

Just better.

Mostly I think they're afraid. I really think they are intimidated or fearful, you know, when something is different, or they don't understand it. And so they mock it, or fight it. I was told once, that you either live in love or fear. I will choose love. No, I don't think it's easier. But why is easier better? Love is just better.

Love is whole. And filling. And cushioning. And forgiving. And kind. True love. True love is kind. I want to live in kindness, not fear. I want everyone to feel that. Some say we should be tolerant. I suppose, but maybe that can feel dismissive, or cold. Or that we should celebrate all of our differences. Celebrating is tricky, and maybe phony sometimes. I say that softly, because I know there must be times when I need to be tolerated, for sure. And yes, feel free to celebrate—anytime. I don't mean that either is bad . . . but there must be something else.

I struggle to find the word, and the only thing I can come up with is just being kind. Kind. For me, I think I'd like that. And I sure hope I give it—the kindness. Maybe then, beyond toleration, without vast celebration, we could just be gentle with each other. Laugh a little more. Live a little lighter. That's nothing to fear. That's something to embrace. That's what is better, not easier, but better. Love is just better.

Chickadee.

"Why didn't you tell me I was small?" she asked her mother.

"Because I never thought so," she replied.

"No really. Am I small?" she asked again.

"You fill my heart with joy. Could anything small do that?" her mother replied.

She smiled. And felt a world of possibility.

"I wish I were beautiful," she told her mother.

"You light up the sky, my love." Her mother showed her the stars.

"What if I'm not smart enough?" she cried before leaving.

"You are stronger than you think." Her mother held back her tears.

"What if *I'm* not strong enough?" her mother asked the open sky.

"I love you," she sang to her mother as she flew.

Love held her. Could anything small do that?

On a cactus.

It's an incentive, for sure, living where I do. You figure it out, you have to, and pretty quickly, how it is you're going to survive. What's going to hurt you. What's going to help you. How you're not just going to survive, but how you're going to live here . . . really live. But that's not unique. Don't we all do that? Don't you? It comes in all shapes and sizes, disguises even, mine just happens to be pretty clear—these prickly things, they're not really hiding. But if you think we don't all have them, then you're just wrong.

We all have them, these obstacles in our path, these things, others, that are going to try to disrupt your day, your life even . . . but that's everywhere. You have to find a way to live with that . . . within that. Maybe you try to make things better, for yourself, for those around you. Maybe you stop looking for the reasons, the answers all the time, and just look for the light.

It's pretty easy to see what won't make you happy when you're sitting on a cactus. But what you (I) have to work for, every day, is finding the good . . . what will make me smile, fill my heart, make this place a little better, for me, and for everyone. What can I do to make a difference? When I end this day, did I add something? I don't know if I succeed every day, but I have to believe there is beauty in the attempt. There is beauty in trying to be kind. Beauty in trying to make this world a little less prickly. I want to be that person. And so I try. And no, I don't mind that I live here. The sun is shining. My back is warm. And I am free. Some days I have to go through the list in my head, of all the blessings I have . . . maybe we all do, wherever we are. This is my home. You are always welcome here, too. It is not an easy place. It has its challenges every day. But it can be a kind place, a forgiving place, and a loving place. If you can see that, offer that, live that, you can live anywhere.

Patience.

Did I learn it? I'm still learning it . . . I hope I'm getter better. Patience. I think that takes a lifetime of lessons. I'm not sure you learn that when you're twenty three and then say, "Oh yeah, I've got it now." I think you learn patience in pieces. You get knocked down a few times, and not only do you learn a little patience, but you get a little humility thrown in as well.

And if you're lucky, the next lesson gives you a little compassion, a dash of empathy. And maybe you get a little smarter and you try harder and longer, and you earn a little more patience. And maybe you get really lucky and somebody loves you, and you love them, and you get a little more patience . . . because you need it!

And maybe you see more of the world, and you see how they see you, and you think, "Oh please be patient with me . . . Please . . . "

And you become more forgiving. And because grace, thank goodness, is so incredibly patient, you become a little more kind. And you give thanks, awaiting the next lesson.

Now.

Sometimes I think I'd like to know the future—how it all turns out, you know—as if that would make it all easier. Silly I suppose . . . and the moment passes. I'm ok with now. Good actually. Skies are blue and my wings are strong. I feel loved and hopeful. Sure I get scared sometimes. We all do. The blue is filled with all those who timidly, nervously, wantfully, stepped out onto a limb . . . held their breath, and took the jump, a leap of faith. And so I love and leap and believe, not needing to be certain all the time . . . feeling there is more comfort in love than in certainty. And would I step out onto the next limb if I knew? Maybe not. Who wants to be stuck in certainty? I want to soar in the beauty of the unknown. It is there I will grow. It is there I will feel. It is there I will truly live.

Fearless.

He's different, right? I mean, he seems different. For the better. You see it, right?

I do. Certainly. It's almost palpable.

What do you think it is?

I asked him.

You did? You just asked him?

Well, it was a compliment really . . . I wanted to know. Just like you do.

So what is it? What changed?

He said he was no longer pretending to be fearless. Now he is fearless.

Wow!

I know, right?

Maybe I'm just pretending. Or, man, sometimes I don't even think I'm trying to pretend. I don't know . . . how? How does it happen?

Maybe it comes with age. Experience. Trust. Some might even call it faith. With time, you might lose a little speed, a little agility . . . but what you gain, in just getting through —there is no comparison. Wisdom. Empathy. You stop worrying about what other people think. And you start thinking about what you can actually do. And you just do it. It's amazing what you can do when you're freed up, you know, from the fear.

I want that. I want to be free. Fearless.

Me too. I think maybe, I mean I really hope, that's how it begins.

Golden.

Sure I love being this color. It seems everyone loves yellow—some might even say golden. But you have to be careful with that, the color, the love. They might love my golden wings, but that doesn't mean they love me. That's a big lesson to learn, for everyone, I guess. It's easy to get your external and internal value mixed up . . . and it goes both ways. I don't think you can truly be loved or hated for your colors, your external. People think they do. They may even act on it, but they are just swinging at the wind. You can't love someone you don't know, or even hate them. We have to see beyond, see what's inside, really feel it, know it. What? Change their minds? No, well, maybe, but it's so hard. It's so hard to change a person's mind. So what do you do? There's only one way really. We have to change our hearts. We have to show each other our hearts.

How do you get them to show theirs? Well, you show them yours, of course. You show them yours.

I can.

"Actually, I can." It had been her response the first time someone told her she couldn't do it. Every once in a while, she reminded herself. It still worked. She flew.

Grand.

They thought they knew me. Coming from here — this small town. But then we all thought we knew, didn't we? What people were like. By how they looked. By how their house looked. The car they drove. Five dollars in their pocket. Their thoughts made me feel even smaller. My thoughts. They were wrong, weren't they? About me. Wasn't there more than this? More. Wait, that was wrong. Who was I to say what was more, or less. Maybe it wasn't less for them. I didn't need more. I just needed something different. I was different. No, that was comforting. It was ok. If I thought I knew what they thought about me, then, maybe I was doing the same thing, to them, and I was wrong. Oh boy, that's messy. I laughed. I really needed to get over myself. And there it was, getting over. Getting through. It wasn't they, (them?) who needed to know my story, it was me. I needed to live my dreams, my hopes, my story, my life. And allow them to figure out their own. We all had one. Have one. Get one. Change it. They're stories after all, not stone. We can all fly with stories, not with stone. So that's what I did. What I do. It's not all figured out. It doesn't have to be here. Here's what I know. The place was small. Yes. But the dream was grand. Is grand. And we fly.

Delight.

"Pink sky at night, sailor's delight . . ." She can't remember where or when she had heard this. She didn't even know if it was true. Was a pink sky better for sailing? She liked the thought of it, and so she believed it.

She could fly in any sky. A bird can do that. But a pink sky, that was her favorite. She imagined herself at sea. Feathers streamed with salt and wet and she moved faster than ever before. Darting through waves of branches and sprays of leaves. She was smooth and hopeful. Her tweet became bubbles that giggled in a pink sky. She rested for a moment on the buoyed branch.

A radio played below . . . *"Birds do it, bees do it . . . Even sentimental fleas do it . . . let's do it, let's fall in love."* Yes indeed, she thought . . . and shook the magic in her wings. She was a bird. She could fly. She was a dreamer. She could swim.

Yes, yes, indeed. Why not love?!
Delightful!

If I can do that.

Sometimes, if you try to take it all in, it can be so overwhelming . . . for me anyway. If I start going through the list of "*I have to do this,*" and "*I need to do this,*" and "*I should . . .*" and "*why didn't I?*" or "*why did I?*" . . . then I'm stuck. So I've learned to release the shackles, and I think this—I basically have one thing to do—lift myself up. Yes, that is my responsibility. I must lift myself up. If I can do that, I can do anything.

I must lift my head, my heart, my soul. I must raise myself to the best of who I am, and then pick myself up again. If I can do that when I fall, I will be strong. If I can do that when I'm sad, I will feel joy. If I can do that when I succeed, I will continue to succeed. If I can continue to succeed, then I will be free. When I am strong, joyful, successful and free, then I really have something to give. Beyond thanks, I can give love.

So I lift myself up, again . . . and again, and higher, and higher still. And I see you, raising yourself up . . . and in full heart smiles, I wonder, "*When did we learn to fly?*"

Seeds.

Words are like seeds. They all grow. You tell someone something good, and they think about it. They smile. And those seeds are watered. But you must know, the same thing happens when you say something bad. And I'm not sure why, but those seeds, man, do they have the power to grow fast.

You can get yourself so entangled in their stems and leaves and branches, and soon, there you are, just stuck in them. I don't want you to be stuck there. I know what they said is hurtful. And it makes me sad . . . well, the truth is, it makes me angry. And I think maybe you need a little truth now.

You need to know that you are really something. And I'm not going to waste my time here saying, "Oh, they're just ignorant, or living in fear . . ." Whatever. What I know for sure is—they are wrong. They are simply wrong. I know you. I see you. I see your heart. You are beautiful, inside and out. Done. That is the truth.

I will never tire of telling you the truth. And I will cut every one those hurtful words down. I will pull out every weed. You are free. They say the truth will do that, and I guess they are right. You are beautiful. You are bound by nothing. The wonderful thing about good words—the good seeds—you can just let them grow. And on the days that you need a little reminder, there they are, in full bloom. Just like you.

Worthy.

The female cardinal is so beautiful. The male gets to be such a vibrant red. So obviously beautiful. The female has to be strong enough to be beautiful from the inside out. To be bold enough to stand next to such a vibrant color and not disappear. I admire that—the strength and courage not to disappear. Sometimes, on the coldest winter day, I'm sure she has the longing for the warmth of a coat of red, but she still braces herself against the steel blue of that winter sky. She knows she is not red. She doesn't have to be.

She is worthy of the same open sky. The same right to fly.

And she is beautiful.

I'm here.

So this happened today. That thing that I thought I'd never survive, well, I'm here. Did it happen the day I started? Somewhere in the middle? Or each day? Each day, gutting it out. Reaching so deep inside, you think you might be beyond the well. Some people will say, "Well, you just shouldn't worry about it, just don't think about it." Yeah, can you imagine, me, not thinking about it? That's funny. Sure, sometimes I actually wish I could just not worry, not care so much. Let it ride. But that's just not me. And that's okay. I have to give myself permission to feel it from my guts. To cry. To over think. To lift each weighted leg with a purpose and make those last ten miles. And then feel the joy of that beast!

So maybe that's how I do things. Maybe you do things differently. We all do. We all can. We all probably should. We're given unique tools, and we arm ourselves. We have our battles. None the same. I'm not sure we really want to hear, "Oh, I went through the same thing last year—no big deal." You know what, that's my deal, not yours—and maybe mine was big. We grow our deals big around here. And you know what else? Feel free to get through your battles, the best you can. Do what you have to do. You grieve the way you want. You take the time you need. You fight the way you fight. And take your victories when you can. You feel the way you feel. Tears and laughter and strength cannot be measured against each other. If you're here, you're doing something right. Use your tools, and live this life as only you can. When the sun goes down tonight, you can smile, or sigh, or laugh, or cry, or perhaps all, knowing you did just fine. You're you—and that's a good thing! And you can think, with a bit of joy, a bit of relief, a bit of your unique humanity, "so this happened today . . ."

An olive tree.

I'm planting an olive tree. My life.

What I mean is, nobody takes the time to plant an olive tree anymore. You need patience with an olive tree. You can plant it and wait five years for the olives, maybe twelve.

Yes, twelve years of nurturing, watering and pruning. The reward is not instant. Ah, instant gratification. I know, I get impatient too. But I'm trying, really trying, with my life, to plant an olive tree. Trying to give without worrying about the pay-off, the reward.

Maybe it's not about the fruit. Maybe it's about the tree. Maybe it's just about the growth itself. I want to have the patience, the beauty, the stamina, the strength of an olive tree. And so I will put in the time to learn, to love, and to live, without measuring the sun, only feeling its warmth. I offer this to you as well. I am here for you.

No abandonings. For you, for me, I'm planting an olive tree.

Truth.

The truth is, I did know what I wanted. Even when I tried to convince myself otherwise. And I can plead a case. I almost had myself believing, so many times. Funny how we can do that. We act so surprised when others fool us . . . huh. Not so surprising, when you think how easily we can do it to ourselves. How great it is when you finally say, you know what, this truth is terrifying, but here it is . . . this is what I want. This is what I'm working for, every second of every day. This is what my brain asks for, my heart pleads for. This is what will save me—the trying to achieve. This is what will save me—admitting what I need. This is what will save me—showing what I love, who I love. And I may be hurt, and guaranteed I will be scared . . . but I already feel whole. I already feel like me. This is my path. This is my truth. That's all I ever wanted.